LIFT THE LIMITATIONS:

19 Ways to Win the Battle in Your Mind
(Second Book in "Lift the Limitations" Series)

GLENDA CARLSON

A WordLife Publication
WordLife Publishing
Dothan, Alabama

Lift the Limitations: 19 Ways to Win the Battle in Your Mind, 1st ed.
Copyright © September 2015 by Glenda Carlson

ISBN 978-0-9987206-0-9

Published by WordLife Publishing
P.O. Box 6673
Dothan, Alabama 36302
Visit us online at: glenda@glendacarlson.com

Front Cover Design © Christine Dupre
cedupre@msn.com

Back Cover Design © Katie Erickson
eemathnut@gmail.com

Illustrations by Glenda Carlson

All Scripture passages are taken from the King James Version, public doman.

Published by WordLife Publishing, P. O. Box 6673, Dothan, AL 36302
Book Layout © 2017 BookDesignTemplates.com

Dedication
To my two sons:
Paris Wayne Walker
and
Brent Alan Retzlaff,
whom I love with all my heart
and pray for daily that they might be:

*filled with the knowledge of God's will in all wisdom
and spiritual understanding,*

*that they might walk worthy of the Lord unto all pleasing, being
fruitful in every good work,*

and increasing in the knowledge of God;

*strengthened with all might, according to His glorious power, unto
all patience and long-suffering with joyfulness;*

*Giving thanks unto the Father, which hath made us meet to be
partakers of the inheritance of the saints in light,*

*Who hath delivered us from the power of darkness, and hath
translated us into the kingdom of His dear Son;*

*In whom we have redemption through His blood, even the
forgiveness of sins.*

according to Colossians 1: 9-14

Table of Contents

Praises for the Book

This book is "A Must Read." Praise God for His Word. He loves us too much to leave us alone! This is a powerful book that keeps one's attention. You find yourself in each chapter. I love the way the reader has an opportunity to accept Christ as their Lord throughout the book. The questions in the back are a great way for a personal check-up. God's ways are not our ways. We must learn to totally trust Him and walk by faith, not by sight. This book will change your life, if you allow the Holy Spirit to speak to you. It's God's amazing grace and simple Truth. Read it and be set Free! I'm recommending this book to all university students and staff.

Jewell-Standford-Bean
Resource Specialist
www.tuskegee.eduTuskegee University

****

"Lift The Limitations: 19 Ways to Win the Battle in Your Mind" gives us hope and encouragement to face life's daily trials. Each chapter reveals Scripture references and life lessons relating to the battles we face in our everyday life. We are reminded we can overcome these battles by keeping our focus on God through prayer, having a strong faith in God and in His promises, trusting Him to carry us through, and praising Him (even through our difficult times.) I highly recommend this book to those wanting to grow in their spiritual faith. It has been a blessing to me.

Jane Robinson
jane.robinson0608@yahoo.com

****

Glenda does a wonderful job connecting with her reader as if she were sitting down having a cup of coffee with a friend, encouraging them in their spiritual and emotional walk with Christ. For new believers, her words, learned from much time with the Lord, will give wisdom and direction and spare them from many valleys and hard lessons many go through in the early phases of their spiritual walk. For a seasoned Christian, she brings a refreshing gentle reminder of the Truth God has given us, what precious privileges we have in Him, and encouraging us to stay the course in our walk with the Lord, even in moments of confusion, failures, anxieties, or weariness. She gives a practical application on ways to WIN the race God has given each of us to win, and to run it with a victorious life! Her book will make a wonderful gift for new believers as well as seasoned believers. We all need to be reminded daily of the practical application she discusses in this book.

Christopher Admire
Christian Counselor
http://www.carpentersrefuge.com
http://irelate.blogspot.com/

****

Author Glenda Carlson, Pastor of two small United Methodist churches in southeast Alabama, has put together a collection of 19 struggles that most, if not all, of us face in a lifetime. These struggles, to name just a few, include fear within our own mind, to unforgiveness, to battles with Satan himself. Reverend Carlson takes us through each battle using her own life experiences. The book reads as if she is talking directly to you in a private discussion. Each chapter is filled with Biblical Scripture. Reverend Carlson shows us the basis of God's love for us through Scripture and His desire to have a relationship with each and every one of us. This book is one you will want to keep handy and read over and over as a guide to help you through life. Whether you have yet to ask Jesus to be your Lord and Savior, or you are a struggling Christian in need of revival, or simply to reaffirm your relationship with God, this is the book for you. "Lift The Limitations: 19 Ways to Win the Battle in Your Mind" will feed your mind and your soul. With God's help you can win those battles.

Amelia Skipper
Chair-Board of Directors, White Oak UMC

****

In today's world of modern technology, and the bombardment of our consciousness with thousands of undesirable thoughts and images every single day, spiritual warfare is for real! Glenda Carlson's latest book, "Lift the Limitations: 19 Ways to Win the Battle in Your Mind," is a great guide for the daily fight against spiritual warfare. Glenda is honest and open about her personal experiences. This, along with the use of Holy Scriptures, gives much hope and reassurance to those of us who have been a bit "more rebellious" and "have had to experience all the consequences of so many bad choices." My first reading of the book brings me back to truth I know, and reminds me of exactly how to deal with current circumstances in my own life! I foresee "Lift the Limitations: 19 Ways to Win the Battle in Your Mind" becoming a personal daily reference.

Diane Braun
Radio Marketing Professional
Wiregrass Radio, Dothan, AL

****

I recommend this book because it is packed with sound Biblical wisdom. Glenda has a passion for God's truth as revealed in the Scriptures and, this is why every piece of advice found here is based on the Bible. She teaches the Word with clarity and conviction, encouraging the reader to keep our eyes on Jesus, stay in the Word, pray without ceasing, and praise God, no matter what. These are words to live by. If you follow the counsel presented here, not only will you win the battle in your mind, you'll live a Christ-honoring, Spirit-filled life, and you'll taste and see that the Lord is good both in this life and the next.

Wayne Davies
www.godwrotethebook.com

****

This was a very interesting book about the world as it is today and, how so many people have lost their faith in God, or simply haven't been saved. I know many young people who need to read this book. It is an inspiration and needs to be read by anyone who is willing to take the time to read it. I am looking forward to reading this complete series. I can totally relate to this book. Bravo, Glenda Carlson!

Paula Bostic

****

God placed this book in my hands to get the Word to me at the perfect time I needed to read it. I have not felt this positive, calm, good, in such a long time as I am feeling now, after reading your book, Glenda. I hadn't even realized how lost I was (how bad my situation had become). Yet, thanks to you and your book, I am not only aware, but have the tools to fix it in hand, thanks to your words, interpretation, and relatable action of the Word of God you provide through this book. Thank you and God bless you!

Roey Bannon Pimentel

****

The author was very thorough in examining every stumbling block that we allow to hinder us in our faith and in life. I especially found the chapter on "Understanding the Brain" to be thought provoking and very informative. I appreciate the author's consistent mention of the Bible as our absolute authority and, the Holy Spirit as our ultimate Guide.

Jennifer Waddle
http:/www.jenniferwaddleonline.com

****

Chapter 1

FRET NOT

Do you sometimes feel like you are just paddling around in a sea of hopelessness? Do you sometimes feel like: "What's the use, no matter how hard I try I just can't seem to get ahead in life? After all, look at the world we live in today. There are so many people who don't even have a job. They can't even support their families like they would like to do. Everywhere I look there are people in despair. There are so many people involved in drugs and alcohol, and in every type of crime you can name. Then I look at the little children and see that so many of them are being abused, or even worse, starving to death. What about human trafficking? This world is a mess. My life is a mess! I am getting so tired of struggling and just trying to keep my head above water."

If this sounds anywhere close to the thoughts that sometimes seem to bombard your mind, then you are holding the right book in your hands right now. This is no accident! You see, God orchestrates it all. We don't understand many of the things that are going on in the world today. We search for answers in all kinds of ways, but we seem to always be falling short of getting the answers we are so desperately searching for.

Please know this: Our God is a sovereign God! He knows everything that is going on with everybody at all times. This is because He is omnipotent (has complete power), omnipresent (is everywhere at the same time), and omniscient (has infinite knowledge). He knows every thought we think daily and every one we will think in the future. I know this is difficult to wrap our brain around sometimes.

However, nothing that happens is a surprise to Him.

We think, "Well why does God let this happen? Why does He let that happen?" First of all, we need to understand that when God saved us, He didn't say, "Zap you are perfect! You will have all the answers you will ever need and they will always be the correct answers to every situation in which you will ever find yourself. You will live happily ever after and you will no longer have any worries, problems, or challenges of any kind." Those types of situations are only in fairy tales. The truth is that the challenges that we go through in this life are there for a purpose. They are meant to help mold us and shape us into the image of Christ. We are imperfect human beings. We will slip out from under grace from time to time. God knows that. We always have a choice as to whether or not to follow the Holy Spirit by inquiring of Him daily about what we should be doing. The problem is most people are ignoring God altogether. Many of them don't even believe that He exists. However, you and I know differently, don't we? We have seen Him work in our own lives enough through the years to know that God is real and that we can trust in Him.

Psalms 37:1-11 says:
"Fret not thyself because of evildoers, neither be thou envious against the workers of iniquity. For they shall soon be cut down

like the grass, and wither as the green herb. Trust in the LORD, and do good; so shalt thou dwell in the land, and verily thou shalt be fed. Delight thyself also in the LORD: and He shall give thee the desires of thine heart. Commit thy way unto the LORD; trust also in Him; and He shall bring it to pass. And He shall bring forth thy righteousness as the light, and thy judgment as the noonday. Rest in the LORD, and wait patiently for Him: fret not thyself because of him who prospereth in his way, because of the man who bringeth wicked devices to pass. Cease from anger, and forsake wrath: fret not thyself in any wise to do evil. For evildoers shall be cut off: but those that wait upon the LORD, they shall inherit the earth. For yet a little while, and the wicked shall not be: yea, thou shalt diligently consider his place, and it shall not be. But the meek shall inherit the earth; and shall delight themselves in the abundance of peace."

God says the wicked will not always get away with their wickedness.

There are consequences to the behavior of the wicked. So, if you are thinking "Well, I can't lick 'em, so I might as well join 'em," get that thought out of your head right now. I hope you aren't having those kinds of thoughts. Even after we are saved, we still have the freedom to make our own choices. Staying in close contact with the Holy Spirit and seeking answers to your questions from Him is the best advice you could ever receive from anyone. I don't care how many degrees some people may have behind their name. For those of us who desire to live the abundant life through Jesus Christ, this is imperative. Why? Because we recognize that pursuing holiness continually helps us to live our life with purpose and we get to enjoy much more peace than we would if we didn't pursue it.

John 1:1-5 says:

"In the beginning was the Word, and the Word was with God, and the Word was God. The same was in the beginning with

God. All things were made by him; and without him was not any thing made that was made. In him was life; and the life was the light of men. And the light shineth in darkness; and THE DARKNESS COMPREHENDED IT NOT."

You can be certain that God will have the final say-so! You can trust Him!

You and I have always heard that His ways are not our ways. It is true! We have a problem trying to understand how He could allow so many things to continue. The truth is, we are going to have to just simply trust Him for the time being. There are many things that we won't have the answers to until we get to heaven. One thing is for sure: we serve a mighty, awesome God regardless of what the world looks like. We choose to believe that God is good. We don't believe God caused all this wickedness. However, we do believe that He takes all of it and uses it for His ultimate Glory. How does He do this? He is bringing people to their knees and they are crying out to Him. This is what He has been waiting for. The Bible says in Philippians 2:10-11:

"That at the name of Jesus every knee should bow, of things in heaven, and things in earth, and things under the earth; And that every tongue should confess that Jesus Christ is Lord, to the glory of God the Father."

Chapter 2

STOP ASKING WHY

I can't help but wonder how many times every person on the face of this earth has asked the question: why? If we had a penny for each time, we would most likely be billionaires, right? Sometimes we find ourselves in a situation and we don't know how we ended up in that particular situation. We thought we were rocking right along, being a good person, making pretty good decisions, and whamo! Something happens to throw us off kilter. We feel like the breath has been knocked out of us. We didn't see the curve ball coming in our direction. You know what I'm talking about. Life is like that!

The truth is that sometimes we get ahead of God.

We know it is His will (what we are doing), or at least we feel in our heart it is, but it just doesn't turn out exactly like we thought it should. We hate to admit that perhaps we made some wrong decisions somewhere along the line. So, we begin to search our hearts and we ask God to please reveal to us where we went wrong. If we will do this with a contrite heart, sincerely wanting to know, then He will reveal to us the answer we are seeking. The good news is we are never too far from God for Him to be able to turn the situation around, and oftentimes He will do it fairly quickly. Sometimes it may take a little longer than we anticipate, but He will turn it around. We are never too far from God that He is not willing to pick us up, brush us off, and put us right back on the path that He has laid out for us. Yes, He does go before us, preparing the way for us. Psalms 85:13 says:

"Righteousness shall go before him;
And shall set us in the way of His steps."

We may get a little bruised when we fall down, but God knows how to heal those bruises if we stay humble before Him. You see, God is looking at our heart. He knows exactly what is going on in our heart. We can't fool Him. That's for sure. He knows if we are sincere or not when we ask Him to forgive us for doing something we shouldn't have done. Well, let's not dance around the truth. He knows when we really mean it or not when we confess our sin to Him and ask Him to forgive us. Yes. SIN! Let's call it what it is. II Corinthians 4:8-9 says:

"We are troubled on every side, yet not distressed; we are perplexed, but not in despair; Persecuted, but not forsaken; cast down, but not destroyed;"

It is indeed a privilege to be able to cry out to God.

In fact God loves it when we come to the end of ourselves and realize that we need Him in every detail of our lives. He loves it when we CRY OUT to Him! He is just waiting for us to get to the end of our rope and He will give us all the rope we think we need. CHOICES! It is all about CHOICES!

I personally am convinced that we can learn to PRAISE OUR

WAY OUT of any set of circumstances. It took me a long time to understand that the longer I stayed focused on my problem, the bigger it became. But as soon as I cried out to God and began to PRAISE Him, the sooner He began to turn my situation around that had been keeping me in bondage.

It was seeing my children struggle and suffer that seemed to cause me the most anguish and fear in my life. Then God began to speak to my heart and teach me that I was going to have to give my two sons to Him and learn to trust Him with them. He assured me that He would take care of them. September, 1996 through August, 1997 was a period of time that I would prefer to just totally erase from my timeline. However, in reality when I look at it from the perspective of how much I grew in my walk with God, learning to trust Him, it was a glorious time. Life is indeed a paradox. 1996 was a major turning point in my life. I had experienced a two year verbally abusive marriage, which was on the verge of turning physically abusive. My two sons were also going through major battles in their lives, thus adding to my emotional challenges. In addition to that, I had to have back surgery in 1997. I was living with my elderly mother and taking care of her at the time. Fortunately, I had three sisters who stepped up to the plate to help me. It was tough to say the least, but God met every need and kept me close to His heart. I learned to fall deeply in love with Jesus. He is MY ROCK, for sure!

Then in 1998, there were many times I would walk the floor and cry out: "THE LORD IS MY SHEPHERD. I SHALL NOT WANT!" It is not a pleasant experience, to say the very least, for after thirty years with silicone running through your system, for one of your implants to rupture. Silicone consists of over forty neurotoxins. I won't go into all the details of that experience because my life story is in my first book *Fear Not: You Have Favor with God.*

Psalm 54: 1-2 says,

"Save me, O God, by thy name, and judge me by thy strength. Hear my prayer, O God; give ear to the words of my mouth".

Psalm 57:1-2 says,

"Be merciful unto me, O God, be merciful unto me: for my soul trusteth in thee: yea, in the shadow of thy wings will I make my refuge, until these calamities be overpast. I will cry unto God most high; unto God that performeth all things for me."

We can never allow our thoughts to line up with thinking that God has forsaken us, because His Word declares that He will never leave us, nor forsake us. We must make a solid decision that we won't allow the enemy to make us believe that lie straight from the pit of hell.

There is no situation or set of circumstances that is too big for our God to handle. We can come through and out of every one of them if we will stay focused on Him and His power, and not try to rely on our very limited self-efforts. He wants to be the One in charge.

God understands when you ask why.

You don't really think that you are the only one who has ever asked that question, do you?

Chapter 3

UNDERSTAND THE ENEMY

I Peter 5: 8-9 says:

"Be sober, be vigilant; because your adversary the devil, as a roaring lion, walketh about, seeking whom he may devour: Whom resist steadfast in the faith, knowing that the same afflictions are accomplished in your brethren that are in the world."

In other words, we have an enemy and we need to be on guard. In fact the Bible says that he comes to steal, to kill, and to destroy. The enemy would like to steal away all your JOY, to kill you, or at least to destroy everything that means anything to you. He certainly does not want you to learn who you are in Christ and understand the POWER you have inside you once you are born again. Once you get a glimpse of who you are in Christ you begin to put that old adversary, the devil, on the run.

Soon you learn of his tricks and how he always uses the same tricks over and over. You learn you must RESIST HIM AND HE WILL FLEE from you. So how do you resist him?

1.   By staying in the Word;
2.   By staying in prayer; and
3.   By Praising God anyhow.

No matter what is going on, you can choose to…

Praise God anyhow!

You may think you can't, but you can. God resides in the praises of His people. That is His home address. So, don't hesitate. Go straight to THE SOURCE of all good and perfect gifts and let Him know how much you are depending on Him and not on your own self-efforts. PRAISE HIM!

Now you know, of course, that the devil would like to cripple you with fears and doubts, right? Yes, that is exactly what he wants. However, we need to keep reminding ourselves of II Timothy 1:7 where it says:

"FOR GOD HATH NOT GIVEN US THE SPIRIT OF FEAR; BUT OF POWER, AND OF LOVE, AND OF A SOUND MIND."

It is true that to fear God is the beginning of WISDOM, but that is totally different than that of having a spirit of fear.

I know what you are probably thinking. Do we ever get to a place where we can relax and just cruise? Well I don't know about that. The adversary is relentless. He never stops using his tactics against us. He will work through people you love and respect to try to distract you. He wants to cause you to get offended so that you will retaliate and get frustrated and mad. I am trying to come up with a way to just burst out laughing when this happens.

Now, don't think I'm crazy. The truth is that Satan does not know what to do when you start laughing. It really causes him confusion because he sees that he isn't getting the desired results that he had intended. However, the best I can do to handle these types of situations when they appear is I simply state out loud:

"Not taking the bait!"

Laugh if you want to, it works. Sometimes I say it more than once. It dissipates the conflict, believe it or not. In the past I have said (and still do sometimes), "PEACE, BE STILL!" These are the words of Jesus and they are very powerful. Try it sometime!

I remember when I was selling furniture at Rhodes Furniture in Dothan, Alabama. I was fairly new to the furniture business. I had sold other things, like insurance and carpet. Anyway, one day all five of us sales people were gathered up at the front entrance of the store, just talking and waiting on some customers to come in and the conversation began to turn sour and escalate. I began to silently pray and ask the Holy Spirit what to do. He led me to say the words of Jesus out loud with authority - "PEACE BE STILL!" Immediately they all began to disperse and went back to their individual desks. That type of atmosphere was certainly not conducive for a customer coming in the front door. Besides, we really weren't supposed to be gathered up like that. We knew better. We didn't do that very often, though because we knew the management didn't like it.

The point is, the Word of God is POWERFUL, more powerful than a two edged sword. We just need to learn the Word of God and stand on God's PROMISES that are in the Bible. We can't have the fullness of victories in our lives without the Word of God. It is like food for our Spirit. We have to have it to be able to overcome the adversary that keeps on trying to destroy us and all our loved ones.

Don't ever under estimate how powerful your prayers are. I believe we have enjoyed a mighty hedge of protection around our nation for many, many years because of Christians praying so diligently. I don't really think that we pray as much as we have in the past. People have become too busy and can't seem to slow down long enough to develop their close, personal relationship with the Lord. I urge you to take stock of your life and begin to set some priorities in your life. You can have a blessed life. But, you have to know who you are in Christ. You have to stay in the Word and you have to pray diligently. All these things are a sacrifice. But no sacrifice has ever been made that God has not seen and blessed.

We need to realize that the enemy is not going to give up. He is relentless. But really, the only thing he can do is slow us down a bit. He really doesn't have as much power as we sometimes think he does. People tend to give him too much power by constantly blaming everything on him and not taking full responsibility for their own actions. Many of the things that happen to us are due to our own actions.

Chapter 4

KNOW THAT FEELINGS CHANGE

Going to the Other Side on the Sea of Galilee
(Photo Taken in Israel by Glenda Carlson)

If you sometimes feel totally helpless, trust me, I do understand. There is one thing we can remind ourselves of, though. In II Corinthians 12:9 it says:

"And he said unto me, My grace is sufficient for thee: for MY STRENGTH IS MADE PERFECT IN WEAKNESS. Most gladly therefore will I rather glory in my infirmities, that the power of Christ may rest upon me."

The word infirmities means weakness, sickness, or even flaws in one's character. Now God is not saying that we should praise Him for all these negative things, but He is saying WHILE we are experiencing all these things we can PRAISE HIM, and when we choose to turn to Him in the midst of our challenge, God is highly honored and He will honor our faith in Him because He will never leave us nor forsake us.

I can't begin to estimate the number of times I have proclaimed the following statement:

Father, Your strength is made perfect in my weakness.

God loves it when we are totally dependent upon Him. You know, there are those among us who have not made nearly as many mistakes as some of us have in our lives. They have always gone to church and been faithful to God. Of course they weren't perfect. But they obviously were much more emotionally mature and therefore they made better choices and never had to experience all the consequences of so many bad choices. The Bible says that to whom much is given, much shall be required. Those of us who were more rebellious and ran from God have much more to REJOICE about, since Jesus didn't give up on us. He kept pursuing us and wooing our heart towards God. We sometimes get so excited about all the things Jesus has done in our lives that it occasionally makes us look foolish to all the other folks. They can't quite comprehend how we can have so much joy in our lives, how we can be so excited about what Jesus is doing in our lives and in the lives of the world.

In Paul's letter to the Romans, he said this:

"For I know that in me (that is, in my flesh,) dwelleth no good thing: for to will is present with me; but how to perform that which is good I find not. For the good that I would I do not: but the evil which I would not, that I do. Now if I do that I would not, it is no more I that do it, but sin that dwelleth in me. I find then a law, that, when I would do good, evil is present with me. For I delight in the law of God after the inward man: But I see another law in my members, warring against the law of my mind, and bringing me into captivity to the law of sin which is in my members. O wretched man that I am! who shall deliver me from the body of this death? I thank God through Jesus Christ our Lord. So then with the mind I myself serve the law of God; but with the flesh the law of sin." (Romans 7:18-25)

We have a dual nature inside of us; one that is bent towards sinning. However, once we understand that and accept that as truth we can gain understanding and wisdom from God as to how to keep that flesh subdued, for the most part, and walk in the Spirit of God. Blame it on Adam, if you want. I mean, after all, Eve was deceived in the Garden of Eden, but Adam outright sinned. We like to blame other people, don't we, for the way we are? The truth is we can't get over it until we own it for ourselves.

When we come to the end of ourselves, we will then begin to live the way God wants us to live. That is, with a very close, personal relationship with the Lord. Jesus doesn't want to just save us from going to hell, but He wants to be the Lord of our lives. He wants to be in every detail. However, He won't force Himself upon you. The Holy Spirit must be invited and welcomed.

So, then we finally come to realize that we came into this world with nothing and we are going out with nothing, and the last dress a woman will ever wear will not have any pockets in it, nor will the last pair of pants a man will ever wear.

WE CAN'T TAKE IT WITH US!

I Timothy 6: 6-10 says:

"But godliness with contentment is great gain. For we brought nothing into this world, and it is certain we can carry nothing out. And having food and raiment let us be therewith content. But they that will be rich fall into temptation and a snare, and into many foolish and hurtful lusts, which drown men in destruction and perdition. For the love of money is the root of all evil: which while some coveted after, they have erred from the faith, and pierced themselves through with many sorrows."

Now, it does NOT say that money is the root of all evil, but it says the LOVE OF MONEY. Money is simply an exchange for a service or a product. It is OK to have money. The more money you have the more good you can do in this world. Bill Gates gives away over 4 million dollars every day. He made the statement recently that he can't seem to give it away fast enough. He is a GIVER! That's why he keeps receiving. God knows the people that He can trust with a lot of money. He is looking at our heart!

Chapter 5

HAVE NO FEAR

This is the very spot in Israel where Jesus said "The Gates of Hell Shall Not Prevail
Against His Church." He was talking to Peter in Mathew 16: 18.
(That's Glenda in January, 2013 in Israel.)
(Photo Taken in Israel by Glenda Carlson)

The Bible tells us in II Timothy 1:7: *"For God hath not given us the spirit of fear; but of power, and of love, and of a sound mind."*

The Bible also says that to fear God is the beginning of wisdom. Who doesn't want more wisdom, right? However, there is a difference between having a reverent fear of God where we view Him with awe and respect, and having a spirit that is afraid to do anything. If you listen to the news every day and stay glued to it, you can become so afraid you won't even desire to go out of your house. You can become very paranoid and suspicious of everything. Yes, we live in a world that seems to have turned upside down. The dark side keeps getting darker, but the good news is: The light keeps getting brighter. I'm glad you are looking and continually going towards the light of Jesus Christ.

There are 365 passages in the Bible having to do with fear. You think God knew that we would be going through some very troublesome times in our lifetime? Indeed! He tells us over and over not to be afraid. With each and every promise He gives us, He assures us that He will never leave us nor forsake us. There is nothing to be afraid of, if we choose to trust in God. However, there is no way people can fully trust God if they haven't read about His promises. The enemy does not want people to read the Bible and find out who they are in Christ and he certainly doesn't want people to know about all the promises God has made to His children.

In our local Writer's Guild the other night, a guy was asking several questions about God, the Bible, and the differences in the North and the South relating to the Bible. He also wanted to know how many of us wrote our articles, stories, or books based on the Bible. I feel like God is heavily wooing his heart, due to the questions he had. I can't help but think that he either may be getting highly concerned about the state of affairs in our nation and world, or he either is on the verge of despair in some area of his life. I could be wrong. It could be total curiosity, but I don't think so, if I know anything at all about human nature. Questions are good. That means that he is interested. When people begin to ask questions, especially openly, then they have begun to seek God for themselves. You see, our spirit craves the Word of God. It needs to be fed. Most people don't realize this, but our spirit needs to be fed the Word of God on a daily basis, just like your body needs food. The enemy has done a good job of keeping this revelation from people for a long time.

When Jesus died and rose again on the third day, He left His Holy Spirit here on this earth to lead us and guide us into all truth. If we have the Holy Spirit we need not that any man teach us anything because He will lead us. Jesus left us with peace also. It is not, however, the kind of peace that you can get from the world, occasionally. But it is a real peace that surpasses any kind of human reasoning. It is the kind of peace that you feel when, even though you may be in the middle of a dire strait situation, you feel very close to the Lord. For example, if a loved one was in the hospital and not expected to live, certainly you would be grievous and concerned, but you would turn to God and, if you are born again, meaning Jesus lives inside of you, then you will feel total peace despite the seriousness of the situation. This is God's amazing grace that John Newton wrote about.

I John 4:18 says:
"There is no fear in love; but perfect love casteth out fear: because fear hath torment. He that feareth is not made perfect in love."

When a person gets up to give a speech, they will tell you that there is an element of fear involved. They chose to DO IT ANYWAY! That's what we have to do. We have to make a decision to move through our fears. Ninety-five percent of what we fear never comes to pass anyway. Recently I heard someone say that the greatest fear we all have is to walk into a room and fear that no one will accept us. This came from a colleague of mine who is a very established pastor with a doctorate degree and he has been preaching to large churches for a long time.

"What time I am afraid, I will trust in Thee. "(Psalms 56:3.)

DO IT ANYWAY!

That is, if you believe that is what God wants you to do, if you are feeling led to go forward. Sometimes we can override God and keep doing things that God doesn't really want us to do, even though it may be a very good thing. Following the leadings and promptings of the Holy Spirit is kinda like walking a tight rope. God knows how to keep us on our toes. That's for sure. We must learn to trust Him. When we choose to have faith in Him and in His promises to us, we honor God and because of that, He honors us by answering our prayers.

And wisdom and knowledge shall be the stability of thy times, and strength of salvation: the fear of the LORD is his treasure. He will be your sure foundation, providing a rich store of salvation, wisdom, and knowledge, and the fear of the Lord will be your treasure, according to Isaiah 33:6. I hope you are saved already. If not, please go to the back of the book and pray the sinner's prayer NOW. Please don't play Russian Roulette with your life! You are first and foremost a SPIRIT, living in a body and you have a soul, which is made up of your mind, your will, and your emotions. Your spirit will live eternally in one of two places: heaven or hell. There are no ifs, ands, or buts, about it. Why take a chance anyway? No need to. What if I am right? I would rather feel secure now with Jesus living in my heart than to get to the end of my life and wish I had simply invited Him into my heart to be my Lord and my Savior and know that I will not spend eternity in hell in continual torture. The spirit feels pain!

Chapter 6

CHOOSE YOUR BATTLES

Muslims are NOT the enemy. The battles are against evil, not humans.
Sometimes they allow tourists inside the Muslim Temple

II Corinthians 5:13-16 says:
"For whether we be beside ourselves, it is to God: or whether we be sober, it is for your cause. For the love of Christ constraineth us; because we thus judge, that if one died for all, then were all dead: And that he died for all, that they which live should not henceforth live unto themselves, but unto him which died for them, and rose again. Wherefore henceforth know we no man after the flesh: yea, though we have known Christ after the flesh, yet now henceforth know we him no more."

Love definitely has a constraining virtue for ministers, being one myself, and also for Christians in general relating to our duty. Our love for Christ will have this virtue. We consider ourselves dead in our sins and trespasses if we are born again (have accepted Jesus into our hearts to be our Lord and our Savior). All those, including ourselves, before we became born again, were lost and undone, dead, and ruined, and would have remained so, miserable for the rest of our lives had it not been for Christ dying on the cross to save us from our wretched, miserable selves.

So, now we are supposed to always act under the commanding influence of the love of Christ. We are to be consecrated to Christ and then and only then will we live as though we are living our life for Christ.

Is this an easy thing to do? No. It is not easy. No one ever said it was easy, but God said it would be worth it. Being a Christian is far from being easy. However, there is one thing for certain: we begin to quickly learn that God is on our side and that He wants to fight our battles for us. We can now learn how much effort we really want to put into WINNING any given battle or conflict. If we try to resolve the battle in our own self-efforts, the chances are high that we are not going to gain much ground in getting the other person to see things our way. On the flip side of that, if we find ourselves in the middle of a situation that seems to be getting out of hand, we soon learn that it is much better to perhaps pull away from the situation long enough to gain some control over our emotions, to surrender the situation to God, and ask for leadership from the Holy Spirit as to how we should proceed in the matter. The Bible says that the Holy Spirit will give you the words to say in the self-same hour, in other words, as you need them. After we have prayed and cast all our cares over onto the Lord, then He will resolve the situation.

Prayer seems to melt away our own fixed and limited opinions on different things and helps us to be able to see a situation more clearly from the other person's perspective.

We are learning to die to self.

Sometimes, after we have pulled away from a situation and turned to God in prayer, we find that we have no desire to try to win the battle anyway, Our desire to maintain the peace becomes more important than to always be right about something. This is called maturing. After a while we realize that our drama has just not helped us to achieve any degree of happiness in our lives.

Of course we are going to have conflicts with our spouse from time to time, especially in new relationships. After you are married, the romance begins to wear off pretty quickly and each person begins to show their real colors. I would venture to say that it takes a good three years to really adjust to the other person and begin to accept his or her idiosyncrasies. The sooner a person or a couple can do this, the better off they are. Men and women think differently and they come together from two totally different backgrounds, having experienced many different life challenges which have helped to mold and shape them into who they are now.

We CANNOT change other people. I don't know why women still think that they can change a man. Some women still believe the scenario, "Oh, I know he loves me. After we are married he'll be different. He'll get a job then" is what they tell themselves. Stop it! Ladies, if he isn't working now, the chances of him getting a job later are pretty slim. Get as far away from that guy as you possibly can.

Sincerely forgive.

In relation to the challenges of the work environment and learning to choose our battles, the way that I would recommend how to handle a conflict would be basically the same as if you were having a conflict with your spouse.

Pull away from the situation to give yourself time for your emotions to relax their tight grip on you and for the canyon of anxiety rushing through your arteries to subside. Go straight to God and forgive the other person first of all. Yes, I said forgive. Not face to face, but in the spirit, in prayer. It doesn't matter whether you are right or whether they are right at this particular moment. Now hear me out. When you make a conscious effort to sincerely forgive the person whom you feel or know has hurt you or taken advantage of you in some way, then is when God can step into the situation and help you. God will NOT deal with the other person's wicked ways until YOU forgive them first, 99 percent of the time.

These kinds of situations happen for a reason. They are meant to cause us to run into the arms of God and seek His help. They are meant to help us to grow in our maturity. After you have simmered down for a while and prayed, then you can maturely and more gracefully handle the situation. This could take a few minutes, a few hours, or even perhaps twenty-four hours or so. That all depends on the given situation and how angry you are most likely, or perhaps some other factors as well. Most of these negative encounters in the workplace are between employees, and management has to be called in to help work through the situation with both parties. Sometimes the situation is between an employee and the manager, in which case, upper management must be brought into the equation.

The point is, we have a choice as to which battle in our life is worth fighting for and we have a choice as to how we will resolve the conflict.

Chapter 7

REPOSITION YOURSELF

You know, most people will not begin to make changes in their lives until they get sick and tired of being sick and tired. Then they finally begin to wake up and say, "Hey, as long as I keep doing this same thing over and over, I am going to get the same results." That's when they have an epiphany of some sort. Their lightening quick mind comes to the forefront and says, "We better do something different." Sure, it takes some courage to break out of your comfort zone, but you know that it is necessary and you've got to do it. So finally you step out in faith and try something a little out of the norm for you and it flops. Your results weren't what you had hoped they would be. Then that failed attempt sets you back in your thinking pattern. You start hearing that voice within that says, "See there, you knew better than to try that to begin with. There is no way you are ever going to get out of this working nine to five just to make a living. You are barely scraping by and you have been doing this for years. You may as well face it. You are doomed to stay right where you are and I really don't know how long you can keep doing this anyway. Times are getting tough and there is no end in sight for inflation. You may as well just give up. It's hopeless!" Does that sound like some of the thoughts that the enemy tries to get you to believe? Some people can get so depressed, that they can even end up committing suicide.

It takes courage.

Yes, it takes courage to take a second chance and step out there again, out of your comfort zone, and try something else. Did you ever think that maybe it just wasn't the right time when you tried the first time? But anyway, you step out, you apply the faith, and it doesn't work out either. That's okay. Take a look at Thomas Edison! Did you know that he made over 1,000 attempts to invent the light bulb before he succeeded? He did not give up. You can't give up. You need to develop a strong resolve that you will not give up, no matter what. You need a tenacious spirit. I am always saying, "It is not in my DNA to give up." I read a book once titled Courage Is a Three Letter Word - Yes. It was all about courage. We have to keep trying. It is far better to keep trying and fail than to just never try at all. We can keep putting one foot in front of the other, keep trying new things, testing the waters, so to speak, and begin to look at life as an adventure. Life can be exciting as your perspective begins to change and you allow your mind to be more creative in its pursuits. When you couple those pursuits with the plan that God has for your life, then you are onto something.

Jeremiah 29:11 says:

"For I know the thoughts that I think toward you, saith the LORD, thoughts of peace, and not of evil, to give you an expected end."

In other words, God knew the plans that He had for you before He ever formed you in your Mother's womb, before the foundation of the world. He already knew everything you would go through and the desires you would have in your heart to move forward in your life. After all, most of the desires He placed there Himself. He wants you to succeed.

II Corinthians 5:16 says:
Wherefore henceforth know we no man after the flesh: yea, though we have known Christ after the flesh, yet now henceforth know we him no more.

There are two things which are necessary to live our lives for Christ. The first one is REGENERATION and the second one is RECONCILIATION.

As Christians, we are told that we are in this world, but not of this world. Well, what does that mean exactly? That means that because we have invited Jesus into our hearts, we have been given a supernatural ability to live our lives above all the rudiments of this crazy world that we live in and still be able to maintain our peace and our joy. We are enabled by DIVINE GRACE. We can learn to live our lives above all the clutter, chaos, and clanging of the world. How? By staying close to the Lord on a daily basis, staying in the Word, staying in prayer, and continually praising Him Who is worthy to be praised. This is the only way we can be regenerated. We become new creatures in Christ, just as the Word says because we have a change of heart. This doesn't happen overnight. But when we are born again, God begins to give us a new heart, one that is more loving, more giving, and more compassionate. As He does, we gain more confidence to keep stepping out in FAITH to try new things, and it is this faith that God honors as the stepping out honors Him. The new man acts with new principles and new character.

Sin causes man to be separated from God. The sinner is filled with enmity against God and God is offended with the sinner. So He appointed a Mediator, Jesus Christ, Who stands in the gap for sinners. Jesus Christ has reconciled the world to Himself. He died on the cross for the entire world. Peace was made with His blood on the cross. Pastors are proclaiming to sinners the terms of mercy and reconciliation, and attempting to persuade them to comply with God's terms because He is willing to be reconciled to us. Therefore, we should also be willing to be reconciled to God. The Mediator, Jesus Christ, knew no sin, but He was made sin so that we might be made righteousness before God in Him. If you are not already saved, please take a moment and go to the back of the book and read the "Sinner's Prayer." God desires that not one of His children perish!

Chapter 8

UNDERSTAND YOUR BRAIN

It has been said that Baby Boomers now fear brain aging more than cancer or even death. People are more afraid of losing their memory and mental abilities than they are of having cancer, heart disease or even a stroke. With the world situation the way it is, people seem to be more concerned over losing control of themselves. People desire to stay mentally sharp and alert. I fall into this category myself.

According to Dr. Eric Braverman, author of *Younger You: Unlock The Hidden Power Of Your Brain To Look And Feel 15 Years Younger,* when your brain is working properly, then your entire body will follow suit. His book is a national bestseller, of course. Recently I saw Dr. Braverman on Christian television a couple of different times, and really all the things he was saying made perfect sense to me. Dr. Braverman is the director of the Place for Achieving Total Health (PATH) Medical Center in New York. He is the author of several books on health, including the best-selling

The Edge Effect, and he has a thriving practice in New York City. What I like about the Younger You book is the fact that it includes an Age Print Quiz, which is a questionnaire for every system of the human body, including the brain. A person can review these questionnaires and present the results to their doctor and be able to talk with him/her more confidently.

I just believe in doing everything one can in the natural realm to take care of our holy temple and leave the rest up to God. He knows how to efficiently add His supernatural to our natural and then we have a WINNING combination. I like that! I know you do, as well. Really the saddest thing in the world to me is to not make an attempt to understand how the greatest computer in the world (YOUR BRAIN) works. If we do make this one of our priorities, I believe it will serve us well for many years to come.

There are habits all of us have fallen into many years ago which after a while begin to take a toll. I am referring to many things that we have been putting into our bodies with no clue as to how they were affecting our bodies, and our brains. The two go hand in hand, of course. For example: fluoride, which is in tap water and toothpaste. It is a heavy duty poison. It calcifies the pineal tissue in the brain and shuts down the gland. You can switch to a natural toothpaste and drink distilled water which helps to detox the pineal gland. Mercury is another poison that will kill the pineal gland. By the way, the pineal gland in the brain produces melatonin which controls the sleep/wake cycle. It has also been referred to as "the principal seat of the soul," or the third eye.

It is not my purpose to go on and on and tell you about all the things that people are putting into their bodies that will eventually catch up with them. Everyone can do their own research. I can surely tell you that I had no choice to begin to do my own research back in 1996 when one of my silicone implants ruptured and not one doctor could determine this. I experienced a collapsing sensation at that time (which I contributed to a diagnosis of pneumonia). A diagnosis was made five years later only after I insisted they be explanted.

As I previously mentioned, silicone is made up of over 40

neurotoxins. Some of these include formaldehyde, epoxy glue, epoxy hardener, and I could go on and on. It doesn't take a scientist to understand that when these neurotoxins are purging through your body for over 30 years, they are bound to be affecting every system in your body, including your brain. Yes, it came out in the original FDA trials that before the silicone implant salesmen took the implants into the doctor's office they were instructed to wipe them off because they had tiny holes in them. In other words, Dow Corning and all the other manufacturers knew that the neurotoxins would be leaking into the bodies of all the women who had them. I have no idea why they had holes, but this is what my lawyer told me. A more detailed explanation is included in my memoir.

The bottom line is that people need to stop and take a survey about what all they are doing to their holy temples. They will only serve you best if you are taking good care of them.

Then there is the EARGATE to consider. Yes. Our ears are attached to each side of our head. We need to guard what messages are going into our brain through our EARGATE. If we allow a lot of garbage in, then guess what? A lot of garbage will surely flow out of our mouths. The Bible says it is what comes out of the mouth that defiles a man.

We also need to take control of our thoughts and our mouths. It all starts with our thought life. What kinds of thoughts are we allowing to infiltrate our minds and wreck our lives? Are we allowing just any old thought that happens to drop in to stay there for a while and kick around in your brain for as long as it wants to? I hope not. You have the power to refuse to have those thoughts. Take control! It does make a difference in your mental and physical health.

CHAPTER 9

LEARN ABOUT NEUROGYMNASTICS

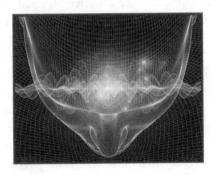

In these perilous times in which we live, it seems like there is such a spirit of restlessness that is causing people to stay caught up in anxiety. Do you ever feel and sense that something is going on in the heavenlies? Do you see people as if they are running around, not quite sure what to do with their lives? We all see the world rapidly changing right before our very eyes. New technology keeps coming to us so quickly that there is no way we can keep up with it all. But we keep trying anyway, and much of it can become very addicting. You can go into any doctor's office, any restaurant, or most any place now-a-days and, if you quickly scan the room, you will see 90% of the people using their phone, interacting with other people with whom they mostly have a superficial relationship. Not all! I said, mostly. What's wrong with that picture? Have we come to a place where we prefer superficiality over real, in depth, loving, relationships where we have real live person-to-person interactions with each other and we relax and enjoy each other's company? Does anyone ever play Scrabble anymore or Monopoly? It doesn't appear that they do.

Have you made it a point to listen to the words that are coming out of people's mouths here lately? They seem to casually throw around the word---stress. Well, what is stress? Stress means to put pressure on, or to treat as important. Now granted, we need a little stress in our lives to keep us moving forward. We need a certain amount of creativity going on in our lives coupled with what we already know and are experiencing. However, if we take a good, long, hard look at what we are doing, we will probably find that our lives have gotten totally out of balance. Stress is very damaging to the heart. Stress can kill you! When you are worried, fearful, or doubtful, there are physiological reactions that take place in your body which can wreak havoc on your mental, spiritual, and physical well-being. A hormone called cortisol is released into your body and an overload of it is not a good thing. There is no way a person can enjoy life with all this going on.

So we have to come to a place where we put on the brakes. We need to slow down and learn how to relax. Take control of your life. This is the only one you will have. Learn how to get your priorities in the right order. However, you don't want to go the opposite end of that spectrum and find yourself caught up in habits of procrastination. This too can and does keep people from really enjoying their life like we are supposed to.

With everybody's stress level off the charts these days, no wonder people are caught up in a perpetuating set of circumstances and they prefer a superficial relationship over a real relationship. People are losing their ability to communicate. They don't want to take the time required to build relationships. Most people don't even understand what is going on in their lives, because they have not stopped long enough to seek God for answers to all the perplexing questions they have. So, they remain in high gear, going through all the rapid circumstances of life and dealing with far more consequences to all the hasty decisions they have made, than they would like to admit.

"Be still and know that I am God..." **Psalm 46:10**

Relax! Enter into God's rest! Slowness is the key! Awareness is becoming conscious of what is going on in your life, in the lives of others, and in the Kingdom of God. If you don't get anything I have said so far, I pray you get this: the yokes of bondage that keep trying to hold you back from achieving your goals and enjoying your life will only fall off when you are in the PRESENCE of God!

Learn to become a conscious daydreamer. You can become aware of all that is going on around you and learn to see everything through the eyes of God. You can learn to bring your life into the present moment. Relaxed attentiveness is key. You can interrupt all those old habits and start to enjoy your life again. Yes, you can even learn to harness the power of daydreaming and mind wandering, as you enter the state of mindful awareness. Reprogramming your brain to the Word of God is crucial to your well-being and for helping you to achieve your God given purpose here on this earth.

CHAPTER 10

KEEP ON PERSEVERING

You know, I decided a long time ago that I was not going to give up. That decision came about when I was on disability for eight long years due to silicone poisoning. Oh, believe me, there were times when I wanted to give up. Many times. In fact there were times when I asked God to just go ahead and take my life. But He kept telling me – *for I know the thoughts that I think toward you, saith the LORD, thoughts of peace, and not of evil, to give you an expected end*, (Jeremiah 29:11). He kept telling me - …This sickness is not unto death, but for the glory of God, that the Son of God might be glorified thereby, (John 11:4).

I was also caring for my elderly mother all those years. If I had given into all the mental and physical pain, what would have happened to me? I kept asking myself that question. Well, the way I saw it was either I would end up in a mental institution or a nursing home because my sisters were in no position to take care of me, nor would I expect them to. I chose to watch Christian television 95% of the time. I felt I had to have the Word of God going into my mind constantly to be able to bear what I was experiencing.

I also knew that God had given me a vision many years prior to this. He called me to be a preacher. My husband had gone hunting for the weekend with our manager from Globe Life, for whom we both sold insurance. My father had died just a few months prior to that time and all I wanted was his Bible. So on this Friday night, just a few minutes after I turned off the light and went to bed, I looked over in the dark to the right and there was a water fall. It was about four feet high and about a foot wide and it looked as if there was electrified water running down the waterfall. Then I heard this voice that seemed loud and clear say to me---"Out of your belly shall flow rivers of living water." I said, "God, that sounds like something a preacher would do". He kept saying, "Just trust me….."

I had no idea what all I would have to go through after that. I won't go into all of my tests and trials here because you can read my memoir titled, *Fear Not: You Have Favor With God*. I do encourage you to get that book. People are reading it three and four times, they tell me. Some are even using it as a devotional because it is full of the Word of God.

You know, I believe the greatest temptation known to mankind is the tendency to want to give up. I am reminded of I Corinthians 10:13:

"There hath no temptation taken you but such as is common to man: but God is faithful, who will not suffer you to be tempted above that ye are able; but will with the temptation also make a way to escape, that ye may be able to bear it."

I had no idea how God was going to ever bring me out of all my circumstances. However, He taught me I that I didn't have to have all the answers all at one time. My job was just to keep trusting Him, just as He told me to many years ago.

So we have to stay close to the Lord daily and keep our

relationship with Him fresh. His Word says that His mercies are new every morning, and that His faithfulness is great. Lamentations 3:22-25 says:

"It is of the LORD's mercies that we are not consumed, because His compassions fail not. They are new every morning: great is Thy faithfulness. The LORD is my portion, saith my soul; therefore will I hope in Him. The LORD is good unto them that wait for Him, to the soul that seeketh Him."

Yes, the waiting is the tough part. We don't like to wait. This generation wants everything and they want it NOW! Mathew 16:26 says,

"For what is a man profited, if he shall gain the whole world, and lose his own soul? or what shall a man give in exchange for his soul?"

If you are a born again child of God, and I pray you are, you have a battle that is going on within you each and every day. We all have a dual nature within us. In fact, we are born into sin, and even after we are born again and have invited Jesus into our hearts to be our Lord and Savior, still this battle continues. The only difference is we now have the Holy Spirit living on the inside of us and, because of that, God is on our side. So we have to learn to lean way over into the new creature that God said we have become. The old man (woman) is still there, and will keep trying to rise to the forefront from time to time, as long as we are in this world. However, because we NOW have the POWER of the Holy Spirit within us, we can choose to call upon Him and He will lead us right out of the temptations that keep coming around. Although the old sin nature keeps trying to re-surface, it does not have dominion over us.

We know and accept by faith that God completely wiped away all our sin when we were born again, even though the nature to sin is still there. So, we have to choose to NOT pay any attention to the enemy, our adversary, the devil, when he tries to remind us of our old self, and tries to make us think nothing has changed.

You can overcome whatever it is that you are going through right now. Keep your eyes on Jesus, Who is the author and the finisher of your faith. Stay in the Word of God. Keep praising God even in the middle of the storm. God loves that. It shows Him that you TRUST Him no matter what is happening in your life at the present moment. Faith is what God honors, and we honor God by having FAITH and TRUST In Him!

CHAPTER 11

CHOOSE TO FORGIVE

Isaiah 1: 18 says:
"Come now, and let us reason together, saith the LORD: though your sins be as scarlet, they shall be as white as snow; though they be red like crimson, they shall be as wool."

In other words, God is always ready to forgive us. All we have to do is surrender to Him, confess our sins, and He is quick to forgive us.

Learning to forgive ourselves is a totally different ball game, for sure. I'm beginning to understand that learning to forgive ourselves is a lifelong process, because the enemy is always right there trying to bring up what all we have done in the past that we know in our hearts was not pleasing to God. Well let's just call it what it is---SIN! The truth where this is concerned, however, is this: who are we to exalt ourselves over what God says? Over the

Creator of the universe? Who do we think we are?

If God's Word says that He forgives us, and it does, and that He totally cleanses our slate, just as if we had never sinned, then we should stand firm on that promise. We should just tell the enemy to go take a flying leap. We have been redeemed by the blood of Jesus, if we are born-again. His Word says, "Let the redeemed of the Lord say so." (Psalms 107:2).

You were forgiven, so you should forgive others.

Galatians 6: 1-2 says,
"Brethren, if a man be overtaken in a fault, ye which are spiritual, restore such an one in the spirit of meekness; considering thyself, lest thou also be tempted. Bear ye one another's burdens, and so fulfil the law of Christ."

No one is any better than anyone else. We have all sinned and come short of the Glory of God, so who are we to sit in the judgment seat of God, and persecute and crucify others? That's not what will bring them into the Kingdom. They need someone to give them a hand, to point the way to Jesus Christ. They need someone, first of all, who will take the time to listen to them and validate their feelings. Isn't that what you also needed? Most of us just want a real, warm blooded human being who will listen to us for a few minutes.

James 5:16 in the Bible says that we are to confess our own faults one to another so that we may be healed. Many people today are suffering from all kinds of sickness and disease that are brought about by bitterness caused from unforgiveness, and I believe that cancer is one of them. Many other ministers believe the same thing.

Ephesians 4: 31-32 says:
"Let all bitterness, and wrath, and anger, and clamour, and evil speaking, be put away from you, with all malice: And be ye kind one to another, tenderhearted, forgiving one another, even

as God for Christ's sake hath forgiven you."

The truth is, God is not going to forgive us if we cannot forgive others. You may want to read the whole chapter of Mathew 7 to get a clear understanding of what Jesus had to say about forgiveness.

Friend, it is not what you are eating that is giving you all the problems. It is what's eating you. Unforgiveness is like drinking a glass of poison and expecting the other person to die. It only hurts us. So, forgiveness cannot be simply an option; it is a necessity, for our own well-being. Unforgiveness causes guilt in our minds and it burdens our spirits down to where we can easily slip into a downward spiral of depression.

God chose to forgive you.

God chose to forgive you when He sent His only son, Jesus Christ, to the earth to die for all your sin, all my sin, and all the sin of the world. He was beaten, bruised, humiliated, chastised, and spat upon, to the degree that is beyond our human comprehension. Why? He willingly laid down His life to take all the sins of the world upon Him, to descend to the pit of hell for all of us. THAT'S THE PRICE OF FORGIVENESS! That's how much our God loves us. He did not want us to go around with heavy, burdened hearts, or walking around looking like we have been baptized in vinegar. God wants us to live free from the burden of sin and enjoy life to the fullest.

So, if God can choose to forgive all the sins of the entire world, why does it have to be so difficult for us to forgive others, especially when it is something we are doing for ourselves? People who can't seem to forgive others are certainly disillusioned if they think they are getting retaliation towards someone for something the other person did to hurt them.

That is such a twisted lie from the enemy!

Don't believe it! Forgive!

Chapter 12

SPEAK LIFE GIVING WORDS

Most people don't realize how powerful their words are that come from their mouths. We are all co-creators with God when it comes to words. Every word we speak is either creating negative seeds or positive seeds. The positive seeds are seeds of faith and are what God honors. The negative words, or seeds, are feeding all the negative situations you may find yourself in at any given time. If you can absorb this chapter of this book, then you are well on your way to WINNING over every situation you may encounter.

Before the human race ever existed, there was only darkness. Darkness covered the entire planet. God spoke the world into existence from the very beginning. He said: And God said, Let there be light: and there was light, according to Genesis 1:3. John 1: 1-3 tells us:

"In the beginning was the Word, and the Word was with God, and the Word was God. The same was in the beginning with

God. All things were made by him; and without him was not any thing made that was made."

God spoke to Mary and told her that she would conceive a son in her womb, and He spoke Jesus into the form of a human being. However, Mary had to first believe the Word of God. She had to believe that she had conceived the Word of God, which is Jesus, into her womb.

My friend, that's the same way it is with us. God speaks to us through His Holy Word. It is up to us to make a conscious choice of whether or not to believe what He is telling us. Now, the enemy will try to make you think what you are reading in the Bible is just a lot of beautiful stories from long ago that just really are not pertinent to your life today. That is a lie from the pit of hell. Recognize who it is that wants to steal away the revelation of the impact that the Word of God can have in your life. Satan comes to steal, to kill, and to destroy. He definitely wants to steal the Word of God out of your heart.

The Bible admonishes us about our words in Psalms 19: 14: Let the words of my mouth, and the meditation of my heart, be acceptable in thy sight, O Lord, my strength, and my redeemer. Psalms 141: 3 tells us that we should ask for God's help in controlling our words: Set a watch, O Lord, before my mouth; keep the door of my lips. In John 6:63, Jesus said, It is the spirit that quickeneth; the flesh profiteth nothing: the words that I speak unto you, they are spirit, and they are life. Proverbs 18:21 warns us,

"Death and life are in the power of the tongue..."

When you really absorb of what God is saying, you will have discovered the main keys to the Kingdom of God, and you will learn how to tap into the storehouse of infinite wisdom and bring God on the scene in your behalf, no matter what circumstances you may be experiencing.

Now, if God's words are life and there is life in the power of the tongue, doesn't it make sense that He has given us the key to create just about anything we want to, provided it is for the good of all and not for evil? Although God gives us these powers, they are a function of faith in God. We read in Romans 10:17: So then faith cometh by hearing, and hearing by the word of God. Our faith is what honors God and God honors our faith. However, faith requires action, stepping out of our comfort zones. Faith is something we exercise when all about us looks like despair. If you have all the answers already laid out for you, then there is no faith. Faith is forgetting all those doubts and doing it anyway.

Faith is believing when you can't see the answers. This is why most people, even Christians, are not receiving all that God has for them, because they think they have to have all the answers already and they are not willing to do anything that is out of the normal status quo.

Well, we have always done it like this!

This is the main reason why churches all across America are going under. They are NOT being led by the Holy Spirit, and they simply do not trust God. When people are led by the Spirit, they are trusting God 100% of the time. They are standing on God's promises, not just singing about them. They are actually exercising their faith and keeping themselves in a state of EXPECTANCY, regardless of the doctor's report. This is faith. This is TRUSTING GOD to the utmost. The report of the doctor may be a fact. However, TRUTH overrides all the so-called facts in this world, any day and every day, always. Remember, we serve a supernatural God and you can trust Him. He is NOT a man that he should lie.

Don't keep feeding all those negative words into your circumstances or into anyone's life. Stand firm in your faith, fully believing in the sovereignty of God, that He is working in the situation and that He is in the process of taking the present situation and turning it completely around because He knows that you will give Him the Glory when He does, and when He does, make sure you do. Give Him the Glory and He will keep on giving you the victories.

Mathew 9: 29 says: *"Then touched he their eyes, saying, According to your faith be it unto you."* It will not be done to you according to anyone else's faith, although their prayers most assuredly can bring you much closer to God. If you are in fear of something bad happening, then you are exercising perverted faith. You obviously are not reading the Word of God and finding out what He has to say about your situation. You are not trusting Him at all.

How's that working for you?

Isn't it time to do the things the way God intended so that you can live the abundant life God wants for you? If the enemy tries to discourage you just quote this OUT LOUD-

"Greater is He that is in me than he that is in the world."

(1 John 4:4: *"Ye are of God, little children, and have overcome them: because greater is he that is in you, than he that is in the world."*) Or perhaps this:

"No weapon formed against me shall prosper."

(Isaiah 54:17: *"No weapon that is formed against thee shall prosper; and every tongue that shall rise against thee in judgment thou shalt condemn. This is the heritage of the servants of the* LORD, *and their righteousness is of me, saith the* LORD.*")*

Sometimes I add,

"I am blessed in the city and I am blessed in the field. I am blessed going in and I am blessed going out."

There is scripture to back up all of this. Do your own research. Do you need to dust off your Bible and read it?

The bottom line is—there are no lazy victorious Christians! Simply work the Word and the Word will work for you. Stand firmly on the infallible living Word of God. Speak His Life-Giving Words into your life and watch Him begin to give you supernatural favor in your life.

Chapter 13

RECEIVE REVELATION

Some things are hidden from the wise.
Mathew 11: 25 says:
"At that time Jesus answered and said, I thank thee, O Father, Lord of heaven and earth, because thou hast hid these things from the wise and prudent, and hast revealed them unto babes."

I often tell people that, regarding the Word of God, it is like it has a protective covering over it and, until a person is born-again, they just can't seem to understand what the Bible is trying to teach them. However, once they accept Christ as their Lord and Savior, the blinders are removed and God begins to reveal things to them that were just mysteries up until that time. Another place in the Bible it says that God uses the simple things to confound the wise, simple things like the act of preaching for instance. We all know that God loves us, well, most of us know anyway. But we, as even devout Christians, find it necessary to come to church on a regular basis; otherwise, we tend to forget how much God does love us. We find that we need to be reminded over and over and over.

So, why do you think that is so? Could it be our fallen nature? Could it be that we were born into sin and that we have a tendency to fall back into our old life patterns? The Holy Spirit keeps pulling at our hearts to stay on the right track. No, God is not going to leave us where we are. He loves us too much to leave us where we currently are. He is always stretching our faith and causing us to step outside our comfort zone.

We are being led.

When Jesus died on the cross He left His Holy Spirit here on this earth to comfort us and to lead and guide us into all truth. So, when we have a tendency to slip off the right path, then He will gently nudge us and pull us back. So, why are we being led? We are being led to learn how to conform to the image of Christ Himself and as we are transformed, we are allowing the light of Jesus Christ to shine brightly in our lives to bring revelation to other people who are drawn to that light within us. Psalms 119: 105 says: *"Thy Word is a lamp unto my feet, and a light unto my path."*

The Bible is God speaking to us. It is life giving and life altering. We really have no idea what we are supposed to be doing. However, the Word of God bears witness with the spirit within us and it causes us to make certain decisions that altar the entire course of where we thought we were headed.

Psalms 19: 11-14 says,
"Moreover by them is thy servant warned; and in keeping of them there is great reward. Who can understand his errors? Cleanse thou me from secret faults. Keep back thy servant also from presumptuous sins; let them not have dominion over me; then shall I be upright, and I shall be innocent from the great

transgression. Let the words of my mouth, and the meditation of my heart, be acceptable in thy sight, O Lord, my strength, and my redeemer."

Many times we aren't aware that we have let the spirit of resentment attach itself to us, or the spirit of anxiety, etc. There is also a spirit of Python. This is a spirit that seeks to crush and suppress people's dreams.

We need the revelation of the Word of God to fully understand who the enemy is, that he has an agenda and that is to steal, to kill, and to destroy. We also need the Word of God to give us revelation of exactly who we are and what authority we have available to us through the Word of God.

"For the commandment is a lamp; and the law is light; and reproofs of instruction are the way of life:…" (Proverbs 6:23)

"All scripture is given by inspiration of God, and is profitable for doctrine, for reproof, for correction, for instruction in righteousness." (2 Timothy 3: 16)

Once we are born-again, the enemy is not going to leave us alone. In fact, just the opposite will happen. However, the truth is that we had all kinds of battles going on in our lives before we invited Jesus to live in our heart. We still have battles, but…

Now we have God on our side,

and He wants to fight the battles for us! Let Him lead!

Chapter 14

SURRENDER TO LOVE

How long have you been trying to accomplish everything with your own self-efforts? How many times have you been so frustrated that you just wanted simply give up, to throw in the towel, to just QUIT? Well, obviously you thought things through a little bit and wondered, "Well, what would I do then, would I just lay around on the sofa all day eating cookies and chips, being depressed, and gaining pound after pound?" Then all of a sudden you came to your senses. You wouldn't be reading this book right now if you hadn't.

You've come a long way. Give yourself credit. We are all a work in progress and we will never graduate from the "School of The Kingdom of God." He is in control. He is a sovereign God and He knows everything about you. He is the One going before you, preparing the way for you to be able to walk by faith into the abundant life. Jesus came that we might have life and we might have it more abundantly, (John 10:10: The thief cometh not, but for to steal, and to kill, and to destroy: I am come that they might have life, and that they might have it more abundantly).

You can completely trust God.

To surrender means to relinquish possession or control to another, or to submit to the power, authority, and control of another. Philippians 2: 6-8 summarizes how Christ was willing to surrender His rights as the second person of the Trinity to the will and purpose of Almighty God. When we stop to consider all the things that we think are important, then we can gain clarity about our need to surrender to God. Many times, all the things that we think are important conflict with God's plans for our lives. This is why so many people are miserable, confused, depressed, and seem to keep making the same mistakes over and over again.

We have been the recipients of many blessings in this nation because others, who have gone on before us, surrendered to God. Have you ever stopped to really think about that? In fact, we have been blessed in this nation for many, many years because of praying Christians who sacrificed their time, talents, and resources in sowing into the Kingdom of God. I truly believe this is what has kept the flood of evil from overcoming us.

We all became too busy.

Then as technology exploded throughout the world, all of a sudden we became too busy to take the time to acknowledge God. We just seemed to not really need God so much anymore. We had all kinds of new gadgets with which to entertain ourselves. This country surely needs to get back to God. He is shaking everything that can be shaken and time is running short. We must get our hearts right with God before it is too late.

It is not Almighty God that is causing all these horrendous things going on in the world today. It is Satan, our enemy. However, God is bringing people to their knees, for He said that every knee will bow and every tongue confess Jesus as their Lord and Savior, (That at the name of Jesus every knee should bow, of things in heaven, and things in earth, and things under the earth; Philippians 2:10).

Willingness to sacrifice is essential to surrendering to God, as we begin to understand that we truly belong to Him and not to ourselves. He didn't put us here on this earth just to store up material things, love our four (man, woman, & two children) and no more, and hand all the material things down to our children. Having material things is not bad in and of itself, but the question is –do they have you? Are they what you long for? We have to come to a place in our lives where we know that we cannot take anything with us to heaven when we leave this earth. We must let go of our attachment to all the material things if we want to live the joyful, grace filled life.

You know, what you do with your life certainly depends on what you feel is truly valuable and lasting. Your god to you is what you focus primarily on each and every day. For some people that is television. For some people it is football. Whatever it is that seems to occupy most of your thoughts, your life, then that is a god to you and that is what separates people from our Heavenly Father. We must know that He is a jealous God and we cannot have idols before Him, if we want the good life, the life filled with peace, grace, joy, purpose, and prosperity.

Sacrificing means putting the Lord first, before any and everything and everyone. II Corinthians 4: 16 says: *"For which cause we faint not; but though our outward man perish, yet the inward man is renewed day by day."*

As previously stated, having faith is what God honors and our faith honors God. When we surrender to Him we are telling Him that we trust completely in Him to handle all our affairs for us. We are telling Him that we don't have all the answers, but we know that He does. We are acknowledging that He reigns supreme over everything and everyone.

Ultimate maturity is when we realize that we are nothing without Jesus Christ and that we can do nothing worthwhile without Him.

It is all about Jesus no matter how you turn the situation around. He is every breath we take! He is life itself and without Him there is no life!

Chapter 15

BE YE TRANSFORMED

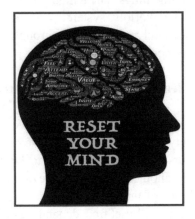

Romans 12: 1-2:

"I beseech you therefore, brethren, by the mercies of God, that
ye present your bodies a living sacrifice, holy, acceptable unto
God, which is your reasonable service. And be not conformed
to this world: but be ye transformed by the renewing of your
mind, that ye may prove what is that good, and acceptable, and
perfect, will of God."

At this point in reading this book, if you have never accepted
Jesus Christ as your personal Lord and Savior and completely
surrendered to Him, I would highly recommend that you bookmark
your spot here and, go to the back of the book and read the sinner's
prayer. Pray that prayer with all sincerity. You will be so happy that
you finally surrendered to God. Then find a Bible-based church if
you don't have one already and begin to learn about who you are

in Christ and the authority and power that has been given to you. The greatest blessing will be that you will spend life eternally with Jesus in Heaven and while you are here on earth, you will learn how to embrace all of God's love for yourself and become a vessel of God's perfect love flowing through you to other people, making a phenomenal difference in the lives of others.

When we invite Jesus into our lives, we are born again. It is at that point that God has plucked us out of the worldly system and worldly ways of doing things. The Kingdom of God works almost backwards from the worldly system. We begin to see things through the eyes of God and therefore, through the eyes of love, learning to forgive more readily, etc.

We are learning how to truly love others...

as we learn how to accept all of God's love for ourselves. In fact, we cannot truly love others until we love ourselves and learn how to forgive ourselves. It is one thing to know that God has forgiven us, but it is another thing to forgive ourselves. Sometimes there are a whole lot of unforgiveness layers to peel off like an onion before we feel totally set free, depending on how rebellious, I suppose, you have been in your past.

We are learning how to overcome evil with good as it tells us to do in Romans 12: 21.

What's in your heart?

Did you know that your heart can be very deceitful? The Bible says so. The one thing that we all deal with almost daily is a spirit of pride and the Bible clearly says, "Pride goes before destruction." We can so easily get puffed up with our own head knowledge about everything, that we can totally overlook what God is trying to tell us. Why does this happen? Because people don't want to slow down long enough to learn something new that will help them to move up to new levels of trust in God.

One scripture I speak OUT LOUD quite often is Create in me a clean heart, O God; and renew a right spirit within me (Psalms 51:10). Discernment is a gift from God that we all are needing more and more in these latter days. If we aren't practicing discernment, which is a gift that must be prayed for and received, then it is easy to allow resentment to stack up in our heart, causing a hard, calloused heart and we do not want that to happen.

Ezekiel 36:26-27 says:

"A new heart also will I give you, and a new spirit will I put within you: and I will take away the stony heart out of your flesh, and I will give you an heart of flesh. And I will put my spirit within you, and cause you to walk in my statutes, and ye shall keep my judgments, and do them."

We will always be a work in progress. After we become born-again, God begins to remove some of our worldly desires and replace them with desires that are more in line with the awesome plan He has for us - the plan that He had for us before the foundation of the world. As He molds us and shapes us into the image of Jesus Christ, it can sometimes be painful, but the pruning is necessary. You see, every negative thing that happens is necessary to help us to grow. These situations are not caused by God, but these situations are used by God to cause us to come running back to Him. This happens time and time again, until we finally completely surrender. This is where He wants us— completely surrendered to His will and to His way.

You are beginning to see the new you.

2 Corinthians 5: 17:
"Therefore if any man be in Christ, he is a new creature: old things are passed away; behold, all things are become new."

Once you begin to see yourself the way that God sees you and start learning to love yourself, then your life will take on new meaning. You will begin to live the truly blessed life that God intended from the very beginning.

Chapter 16

CONTROL YOUR SPIRIT

We are living in a time where there seems to be a spirit of restlessness everywhere you turn. The speed at which new technology is emerging is astounding to say the least. People's attention span is shorter than it has ever been. It takes a lot, first of all, to get their attention, and it takes a lot to keep their attention. It looks as though a spirit of anxiety is trying to cripple the nation, and the world.

Be anxious for nothing.

What I am finding most helpful in such a time as this is to quote OUT LOUD, as many times a day as necessary Philippians 4: 6-7, personalizing it for my own well-being like this:

I am anxious for nothing, but in everything by prayers of praise and thanksgiving, with supplications I make my requests known unto God, And the peace of God, which passeth all understanding, keeps my heart and my mind in Christ Jesus.

When I do this I can immediately feel my spirit calming down. Quoting Psalms 23 OUT LOUD is also an awesome way to calm down your spirit. Out spirit craves the Word of God. I can't say that enough. Reading Psalms 23 is better than visiting 30 psychiatrists. So, next time you feel that resentful attitude, or anxiety emerging within, turn to those scriptures, and bring life back to your spirit. You will find that learning to speak God's Word to your spirit has tremendous benefits for you. He said His words are spirit and they are life to those that find them.

Keep your eyes on Jesus, Who is the author and the finisher of your faith. Satan wants you to keep your eyes on the problem. But, if you do, then the problem will multiply and you don't want that to happen.

Fix your eyes on Jesus and feast from the table of God, so that you can once again learn to enjoy life the way God intended you to. Recognize that the enemy does not want you to read your Bible, and he certainly does not want you to quote any scriptures, especially OUT LOUD where others may hear and begin to experience blessings in their lives, as well.

You are learning all the tactics of the enemy who comes to steal, kill, and destroy. But Jesus came that you might have life and you might have it more abundantly. Glory to God!

Set your affection on things above.

2 Peter 1: 4-9:

"Whereby are given unto us exceeding great and precious promises: that by these ye might be partakers of the divine nature, having escaped the corruption that is in the world through lust. And beside this, giving all diligence, add to your faith virtue; and to virtue knowledge; And to knowledge temperance; and to temperance patience; and to patience godliness; And to godliness brotherly kindness; and to brotherly kindness charity. For if these things be in you, and abound, they make you that ye shall neither be barren nor unfruitful in the knowledge of our Lord Jesus Christ. But he that lacketh these things is blind, and cannot see afar off, and hath forgotten that he was purged from his old sins".

In other words, we should always keep our eyes on Jesus. When we do, the cares of this world grow strangely dim, as God fights the battle for us and resolves every issue, leading us and guiding us along the way.

I Corinthians 9: 26-27:
"I therefore so run, not as uncertainly; so fight I, not as one that beateth the air: But I keep under my body, and bring it into subjection: lest that by any means, when I have preached to others, I myself should be a castaway".

Your discipline is now going deeper.

James 1:19: "Wherefore, my beloved brethren, let every man be swift to hear, slow to speak, slow to wrath:…"

What we do want, for sure, is enough control over our own spirit that we do not react to others when they are doing things that seem to rub us the wrong way. Instead, we are learning to pull back (call time out), re-fresh ourselves in prayer, surrender the situation to God, and allow the Holy Spirit to lead us. He will show us precisely the right way to handle each and every situation we face in a godly manner. We have to recognize that the enemy wants us to get offended easily so that we will react and cause the situation to escalate.

Chapter 17

DRAW CLOSER TO GOD

God is constantly wooing our hearts to come to Him. When Jesus rose that third day from the dead, He left His Holy Spirit here on earth to comfort us and to lead and guide us into all truth. However, He does not force Himself upon us. He gives us a choice, as to whether or not we want to take the time to come into His presence. In His presence is fullness of joy. It is in the presence of God where all the yokes of bondage are broken off of us, and where the mental, physical, spiritual, and financial chains are broken. How can this be? Because God is forever trying to get us to the end of ourselves. He is doing everything He possibly can to get us to give up all the self-efforts and to trust Him.

Does that mean that we just sit down and leave everything up to Him? Not by a long shot. He fully expects us to occupy until Jesus comes for us (His bride). That means to work or to stay busy doing something worthwhile that will benefit others as well as yourself.

You see, God wants to be in all the details of your life.

He wants to do the leading with His Holy Spirit because He knows that His way is the best way and His way will bring to you far greater blessings than what we ourselves can conjure up in our own self efforts.

Isaiah 55:1-3:

"Ho, every one that thirsteth, come ye to the waters, and he that hath no money; come ye, buy, and eat; yea, come, buy wine and milk without money and without price. Wherefore do ye spend money for that which is not bread? and your labour for that which satisfieth not? hearken diligently unto me, and eat ye that which is good, and let your soul delight itself in fatness. Incline your ear, and come unto me: hear, and your soul shall live; and I will make an everlasting covenant with you, even the sure mercies of David."

Our spirits crave the Word of God.

Most people don't realize that. We are first and foremost a spirit with a mind, living in a body. Just as surely as the body has to be fed with food, the Word of God is necessary food for our spirits. The Word of God has supernatural life-giving properties to it. It is a living Word and when we speak His Word, it comes alive in our lives, bringing God's best into our situations, and He always wants the very best for us.

Isaiah 55: 6-9:

Seek ye the Lord while he may be found, call ye upon him while he is near: Let the wicked forsake his way, and the unrighteous man his thoughts: and let him return unto the Lord, and he will have mercy upon him; and to our God, for he will abundantly pardon. For my thoughts are not your thoughts, neither are your ways my ways, saith the Lord. For as the heavens are higher than the earth, so are my ways higher than your ways, and my thoughts than your thoughts.

In Psalms 145, God tells us that He is near to all them that call on Him and that He will fulfill their desire if they fear Him. This, of course, is a reverent type of fear, not one where we feel like He is about to knock us out with a baseball bat if we mess up.

We are to serve God with gladness.

According to Psalms 100, to worship Him, sing to Him, and to know that we belong to Him. We do not belong to ourselves. He purchased us with the blood of Jesus. We, who have asked Jesus to be our Lord and Savior, are His children and we belong to Almighty God. He constantly reminds us that He wants to be first place in our lives.

In Hebrews 10, the Word speaks of the sacrifices they had previously given to God with the burnt offerings of animals. These were done under the law, (the Ten Commandments) which proved ineffective for the people, since they were unable to make all the atonements for all their sin in their own self-efforts. This is why God had to manifest Himself in the form of a human being (Jesus Christ) and come to earth and die on a cross for all the sins of mankind.

Jesus came and willingly laid down His life for the ransom of the whole world. He died for every sin we have ever, or ever will commit. But this does not give us a license to sin, because sin always has consequences. Many people today think they are getting away with all the evil they are involved in, but the truth is: they are not getting away with anything. God will have the last say in the matter.

Chapter 18

BE STRENGTHENED
WITH POWER

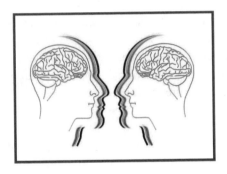

Christians realize that we are indeed in a major spiritual battle each and every day of our lives. They know that Satan and all his little demons are trying to destroy humanity any way they can. They will try to destroy anyone they can to keep them from having a close relationship with our Heavenly Father.

This is Spiritual Warfare! 2 Corinthians 10:4 says: *"For the weapons of our warfare are not carnal, but mighty through God to the pulling down of strongholds."*

The first battle was in the Garden of Eden and because of the fall of Adam and Eve, Satan has been trying to destroy mankind ever since. However, God empowers us through His Word and shows us how to defeat the enemy. Our weapons are not normal, but they have divine power to destroy anything the enemy throws at us.

Ephesians 1:3:

"Blessed be the God and Father of our Lord Jesus Christ, who hath blessed us with all spiritual blessings in heavenly places in Christ:…"

Almighty God fights the battles for us through His living Word, but WE MUST SPEAK WHAT GOD SAYS IN HIS WORD, in order to bring Him on the scene in our behalf.

Ephesians 6: 11:

"Put on the whole armour of God, that ye may be able to stand against the wiles of the devil." God warns us about the devil, but He gives us the clothes that we are to wear daily in order to fight to win. If we choose to clothe ourselves appropriately, then we will be able to overcome the enemy, Satan.

Ephesians 6:12:

"For we wrestle not against flesh and blood, but against principalities, against powers, against the rulers of the darkness of this world, against spiritual wickedness in high places."

This is what spiritual warfare is all about. Our fight is NOT against other people, but against the evil spirits that seek to divide us against other people. We can confidently fight all the battles if we keep our armor on.

Rekindle your faith daily.

When we rekindle our faith on a daily basis, we feel more gratitude, generosity, and love towards ourselves and towards others, as well. So, we must learn to

Feed your faith, not your fear.

The following is how I PERSONALIZE these scriptures and they mean more to me. You may like to do this too.

✓ Philippians 4: 6-7:

I am careful for nothing; but in every thing by prayer and

supplication with thanksgiving I let my requests be made known unto God. And the peace of God, which passeth all understanding, keeps my heart and mind through Christ Jesus.

✓ I Peter 5: 6-7:
I humble myself therefore under the mighty hand of God, that he may exalt me in due time: Casting all my care upon him; for he careth for me.

✓ Psalm 34: 17-19:
I am righteous through the blood of Jesus and I cry, and the LORD heareth, and delivereth me out of all my troubles. The LORD is nigh unto me when I have a broken heart; and saveth such as be of a contrite spirit. I have many afflictions, but the Lord delivereth me out of them all.

✓ Psalms 112: 6-8:
Surely l am not moved for ever: the righteous shall be in everlasting remembrance. I am not afraid of evil tidings: my heart is fixed, trusting in the Lord. My heart is established, I shall not be afraid, until I see my desire upon my enemies (my thoughts).

✓ Romans 8: 31:
What shall I then say to these things? If God be for me, who can be against me?

✓ Proverbs 3: 5-6:
I trust in the LORD with all my heart; and lean not unto my own understanding. In all my ways I acknowledge him, and he directs my paths.

✓ Isaiah 41: 10:
I Fear not; for God is with me : I am not dismayed; for He is my God: He strengthens me; yea, I helps me; yea, He

upholds me with the right hand of His righteousness.

Friend, you are getting a better understanding about the battle we all find ourselves in daily, and you are being equipped to supernaturally stand firm right in the middle of the battle. Speaking God's Words are powerful. But, guess who doesn't want you to even pick up the Bible and read them, much less quote them out loud, or memorize them. I would highly recommend that you read these scriptures daily. Then take one scripture every week and memorize it. Write it on a 3 x 5 card and stick it on your refrigerator. Plant the Word in your heart so that no devil can defeat you in the next storm. Be strengthened with the power of His might!

Chapter 19

FIND UNMERITED FAVOR

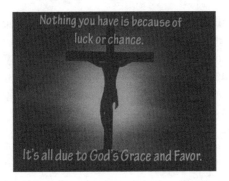

Jesus is infinitely interested in your total well-being. He is interested in every detail of your life. None of what you go through is insignificant to Him. He will never discount anything that you may seek Him for as being too petty, and you can talk to Him about anything that is on your heart at any given moment of time. His tenderness and strength is wrapped up all together.

Jesus is 100 percent man and at the same time 100 percent God. As man, he understands everything that you have gone through, are presently going through, or ever will go through in the future. So you need to know that God is on your side with His authority and all of His resources to help you any time you call on Him.

He loves you and accepts you just as you are. However, He loves you too much to leave you as you are. But He does not condemn you. He loves you perfectly. When you finally believe that and accept that as truth, then you will know that it truly is unmerited favor that He gives to us, that we do not deserve, nor can you ever earn for yourself.

We can go about our life in two different ways. One is to depend upon our own self-efforts. The other is to depend completely on the unmerited favor and blessings of God. To me it is a no-brainer. I lean strongly on His unmerited favor in every area of my life. If you depend on deserved favor, you are certainly cutting yourself off from the full blessings of God. Besides, that is the way of the world. If you are born-again, you are in the world, but you are not of the world.

God's unmerited favor comes through His grace and by the power of what was accomplished on the cross at Calvary 2000 years ago. This goes entirely against every worldly system upon which you have ever depended. Every success, opportunity, blessing, or breakthrough, no matter what it is, comes by His unmerited favor. You don't need to do anything to qualify for His blessings. They are yours automatically. All you have to do is to receive them. All things are yours through the blood of Jesus Christ. If you think that you have to do this or do that, then you are living under legalism, and you are not receiving the full measure of God's grace and what Jesus died to give to us.

Many of the people who insist on requirements being met are loving and very sincere people. But in reality, they are pointing people back to the old law, the Ten Commandments, whether they realize it or not. When Jesus came to die for us, and we became born-again, we came under the dispensation of grace. We are no longer under the Law. God saw that we, as human beings, were unable to keep all those old laws and do all the atonements and sacrifices that were expected. It was just too much.

That's why He came up with His second plan and that was to manifest Himself in the form of a human being, His own Son, Jesus Christ, to come to earth to die for us. That's how much He loves us. We are no longer under the Old Covenant of Law. We are NOW under grace.

The new covenant that we are under is based completely upon Jesus dying on the cross at Calvary 2000 years ago and upon the shed blood of Jesus Christ Who died once and for all of mankind. It is all about having a personal relationship with the Lord based on receiving what God Himself did for us many years ago. When we fully receive what He has done, we will live and move and have our being in God, and that is in LOVE. Love is all that matters.

When we are under grace we effortlessly super-exceed the expectations of the Law of Moses. In the Amplified Bible in 2 Peter 1: 2 says:

"May grace (God's favor) and peace (which is perfect well-being, all necessary good, all spiritual prosperity, and freedom from fears and agitating passions and moral conflicts) be multiplied to you in (the full, personal, precise, and correct) knowledge of God and of Jesus our Lord."

This unmerited favor of God will flow like rivers of living water into every dry area of your life, whether it is your physical body, your marriage, your career, or your finances, when you see Jesus! God's unmerited favor will surely increase more and more, as you grown in the knowledge of His finished work at the cross.

So, do you want to have success beyond your natural intelligence, qualifications, and ability? Of course, you do. We all do!

God's unmerited favor is the gospel.

When you have Jesus you have unmerited favor! If you don't know Him as your Lord and Savior, I pray you will not go to bed tonight without inviting Him into your heart to be your Lord and Savior. He loves you. He died for you. Had you been the only one in the whole world, He still would have died for you. That's how much God loves you!

Grace is the undeserved, unearned, and unmerited favor of Almighty God! You can begin to depend on His unmerited favor for success in every area of your life.

"In the Midst of My Rebellion"

I learned about You as a child
I accepted You as my Lord and Savior
However, not too many years later
I wandered off into the wilderness
Even in the midst of my rebellion
I sometimes felt Your presence
It was the essence of Your being
My heart was surely longing for
I seemed to sense within my spirit
There must be more to life
Than what my present experience
Afforded me at that time and place
You invaded my space
Even in the midst of my rebellion
I didn't know of any plan
That You could have for me
But I could see You had no
Intentions of leaving me alone
The songs we used to sing
Would sometimes infiltrate my mind
Jesus loves me would ring loudly
In my ears and my fears would
Somehow, subside, if even for a short time
In the midst of my rebellion

The Sinner's Prayer

Father, I come humbly before You and I confess to You that I am a sinner in need of a Savior. Please forgive me of all my sins. Wash me and cleanse me. I know now that I have hurt You and I ask You to forgive me.

Jesus, I choose right here and right now to believe that You came to earth and willingly laid down Your life for the sins of the whole world. Come into my heart now and be the Lord of my life, as well as my Savior.

Fill me to overflowing with Your Holy Spirit and help me to know that You are always with me.

Lead me and guide me and help me to make wise choices for my life. Help me to forgive others as you have forgiven me.

Show me the plan God has for me. I surrender all that I am to You. Thank You for loving me enough to die for me.

In Jesus' name, Amen!

"The Crucifixion"
Painting by Glenda Carlson

Questions to Help You Grow

I would suggest that you grab a pen and notebook and take the time to honestly answer the questions below. I promise you that you will be glad you did.

1. Can you identify what it is that seems to keep pulling you back from making any attempts to reach for your dreams?
2. What is it that tries to make you feel you aren't worthy of having a better life than what you are desiring?
3. Can you be totally honest with yourself and search your heart to discover whether or not you are harboring any unforgiveness towards anyone for anything, including yourself?
4. Are you stopping to examine your choices when things seem to go wrong for you?
5. Are you spending time alone with God on a regular basis?
6. To what extent do you know that the enemy wants to destroy every dream that you have?
7. What kinds of ways have you developed to get back on track with your faith when you have made unwise decisions?
8. How do you see the world all around you? Do you see the good, or just the bad?
9. How important is it for you to always be right about everything?
10. In what ways are you working with the Holy Spirit for Him to chisel off a few rough character traits that may still be trying to hold on?
11. How important is it you understand that your brain is one of the most complex organs of the body and needs desperately to be reprogrammed?
12. When you experience down times, do you tend to focus on everything in your life that has ever gone wrong, or draw strength from what the Lord has pulled you through before?
13. Do you purposely seek to keep your heart clean before the

Lord every day, knowing that resentment can spring up quickly, and if so, how?

14. What kind of conversation are you having with yourself on a regular basis?

15. Are you open to receive constructive advice or does it always have to be your way or the highway?

16. Are you examining yourself regularly to discover whether or not you are growing spiritually as we all should?

ABOUT THE AUTHOR

Glenda Carlson is on a mission to help you become all that God wants you to be, using your own God-given talents and abilities to impact the world. She believes it's your time to let your light SHINE !

Glenda has been in the ministry since 2007 and is presently serving two small Methodist churches in Alabama. She has been taking courses at Birmingham Southern in Birmingham, Alabama as well as some at Huntingdon College in Montgomery, Alabama. She will soon have all the courses completed and she has consistently maintained a "B" average, and even two or three "A" grades.

In 2013, Glenda was one of 26 local Methodist Pastors who were privileged enough to go to Israel on a nine day intensive Bible Study Tour in Israel. This was not just any run of the mill tour in the Holy Land, but one where they had Bible Scholars on site teaching them. It was said by the Alabama Course of Study Director, Dr. Walter Cash, that to him this tour was equal to one year in Seminary. Glenda agrees with Dr. Cash!

Glenda enjoys interjecting energy and enthusiasm into the hearts of the people she touches, helping them to trust God completely and to reach for their dreams, as she helps them to embrace all His love and develop their personal walk with the Lord at new and exciting levels!

If you are ready to go to the next level, check out
Glenda's Website:

glenda@glendacarlson.com

You can also find her on Facebook at:
https://www.facebook.com/glenda.carlson.5

As well as on Twitter at:
https://twitter.com/carlson_glenda

Amazon Author Page:
www.amazon.com/author/amazonauthor-glendacarlson

Pinterest: https://www.pinterest.com/littlezig/

You Tube: http://tinyurl.com/03zM392

Google Plus: http://tinyurl.com/nra6Yb3

Disclaimer:

There is no promise or representation that you will achieve precisely the life you are desiring.

The truth is, it takes a lot of work, along with a closer walk with the Lord, allowing Him to change us from the inside out. The use of the information contained in this book should be based on your own due diligence, and you agree that we are not liable for your success or failure.

REFERENCES

The Holy Bible, King James Version, public domain.

Dr. Eric Braverman, author of *Younger You: Unlock the Hidden Power of Your Brain.*

Photo of Boat & Cave---Taken in Israel by Glenda Carlson

Photo of Muslim Temple - Taken in Israel by Glenda Carlson

Crucifixion Painting - Glenda Carlson

Most of the Images-Fotolia

Front Cover Design © Christine Dupre
cedupre@msn.com

Back Cover Design © Katie Erickson
eemathnut@gmail.com

MAY I ASK A FAVOR ?

While it is fresh on your mind, would you please take a couple of minutes and go to the following link and give us an honest review at

www.amazon.com/author/amazonauthor-glendacarlson

Just search for the this book title to leave a review. You will be tremendously helping to enhance a lot of other people's lives and perhaps even save some lives.

It is Glenda's heartfelt prayer that you have been touched personally by what you have read in this book and she is certain that you feel the same way as she does about helping other people.

Jesus Christ is returning soon! Let's help as many people as we possibly can! We do honestly need your help, because we know we cannot do it alone. We are very thankful that you have taken your time to read this book and we feel in our heart that you will want to share it with others.

SPEAKING THE "AARONIC BLESSING" OVER YOU

"MAY THE LORD BLESS YOU AND KEEP YOU. MAY THE LORD MAKE HIS FACE TO SHINE UPON YOU AND BE GRACIOUS UNTO YOU. MAY THE LORD LIFT UP HIS COUNTENANCE UPON YOU AND GIVE YOU PEACE."

CONCLUSION

Now that you have finished reading LIFT THE LIMITATIONS: 19 Ways to Win the Battle in Your Mind, I hope that you have taken the time to answer the "Questions To Help You Grow" at the end. When someone has encouraged you, it is then time to take ACTION on some things you have learned, in order to come out of your stale comfort zone. Life is made up of changes and we are either willing to work with the Holy spirit and allow Him to help us change, or we will be suffering the consequences of our own disobedience. God desires you to come up to a new level in Him.

So, take a deep breath! Breathe in new found courage and freedom to step out of your comfort zone and GO FOR IT! You only have one life. Live it to the fullest!

If you are interested in reading other books by Glenda Carlson you can visit her website at:

glenda@glendacarlson.com

*Remember this is only the second book in the series of "Lift the Limitations." The first one is *Jesus Knocking: Enjoy Life Abundantly.*

May God richly bless you with His supernatural Divine Favor!